ivy

Powerful Magical Touch

Text © 2022 by Kim Magraw
Illustrations © 2022 by Taimani Emerald Reed
ISBN-13: 978-1-942369-75-2
ISBN-10: 1-942369-75-1
First Edition 2022 © Ivy
casasolaeditores.com

All rights reserved. No part of this publication may be reproduced or transmitted in any form or by any means without the express written consent of the publisher.

Cover Design: Knny Reyes
Layout and editorial care: Óscar Estrada

Printed in the United States of America

info@casasolaeditores.com

POWERFUL MAGICAL TOUCH

KIM MAGRAW

Illustrations by TAIMANI EMERALD REED

POWERFUL MAGICAL TOUCH

KIM MAGRAW

illustrations by TAIMANI EMERALD REED

I'm Trina. I just turned 8.

There's Mom holding me when I was brand new.

That's my brother Cole holding my hand as we cross the street.

There's Dad holding Grandpa's hand when he was very sick.

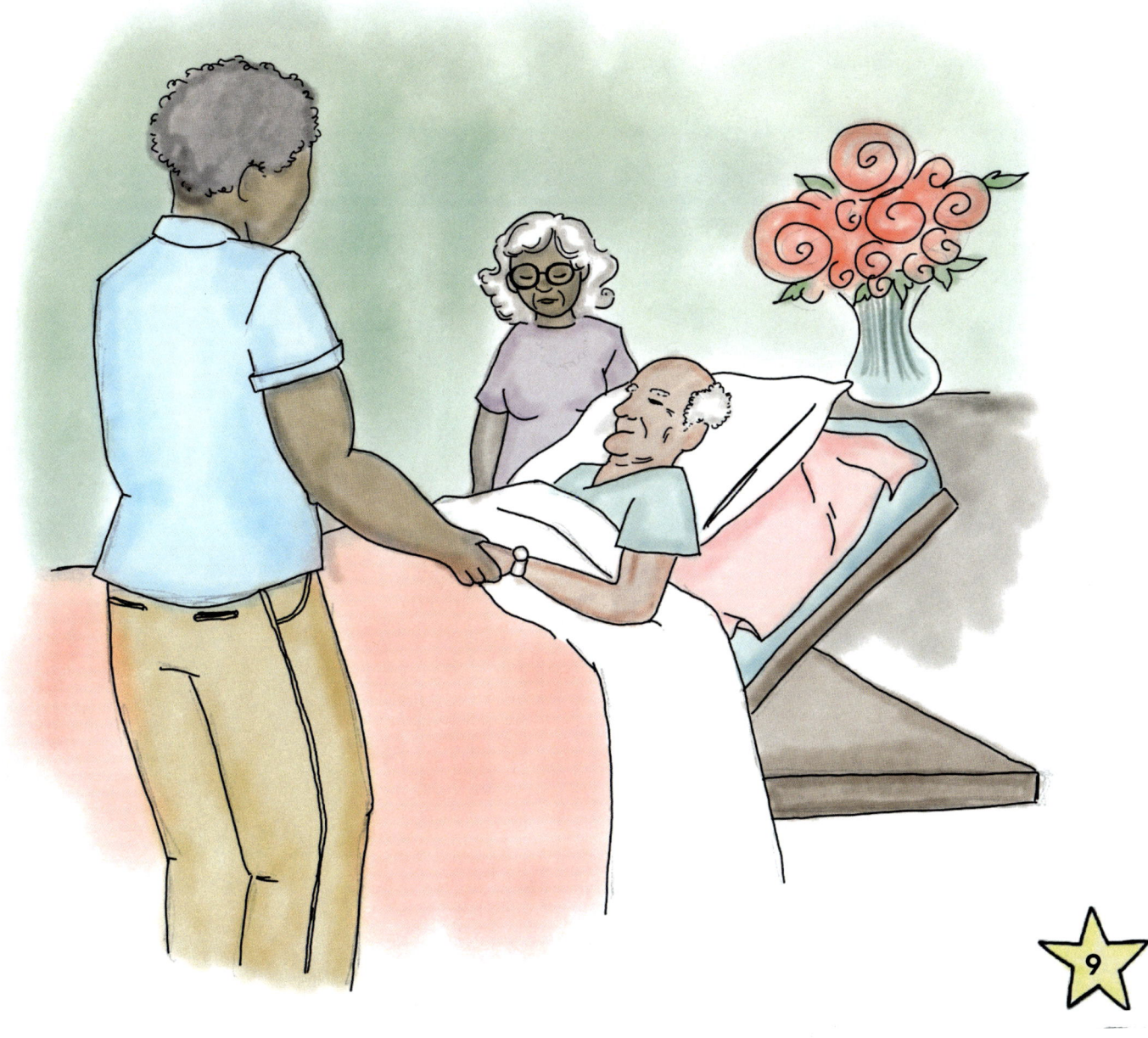

Dad says everyone needs touch, from our first day until our very last.

Dad is a massage therapist. That means he knows a lot about how powerful and magical touch can be.

Dad taught me that I can say special things with my touch to other people and even animals.

I LOVE YOU.

With touch I can even say things
there are no words for.

When I touch someone I can make them joyful. I can help them relax and I can help them do more. And they can do the same for me.

Anyone who touches us must have **three gold stars**.

Gold star number one:
They must have our trust.

Trust means I know them well and I know they want me to be safe and happy. Because I'm eight years old Mom and Dad help me decide who gets the golden star of trust.

Dad says everyone should have a Trust Team. What is a Trust Team? It's the people I trust who I can talk to about any touch. For me it's Dad and Mom, my Grandma, and my teacher Miss Gruder.

Gold star number two:
We give our consent.

CONSENT

If I don't want to be touched or I'm not sure, that means STOP.

Sometimes Cole doesn't want to be touched and I have to stop, even when I really want to poke him.

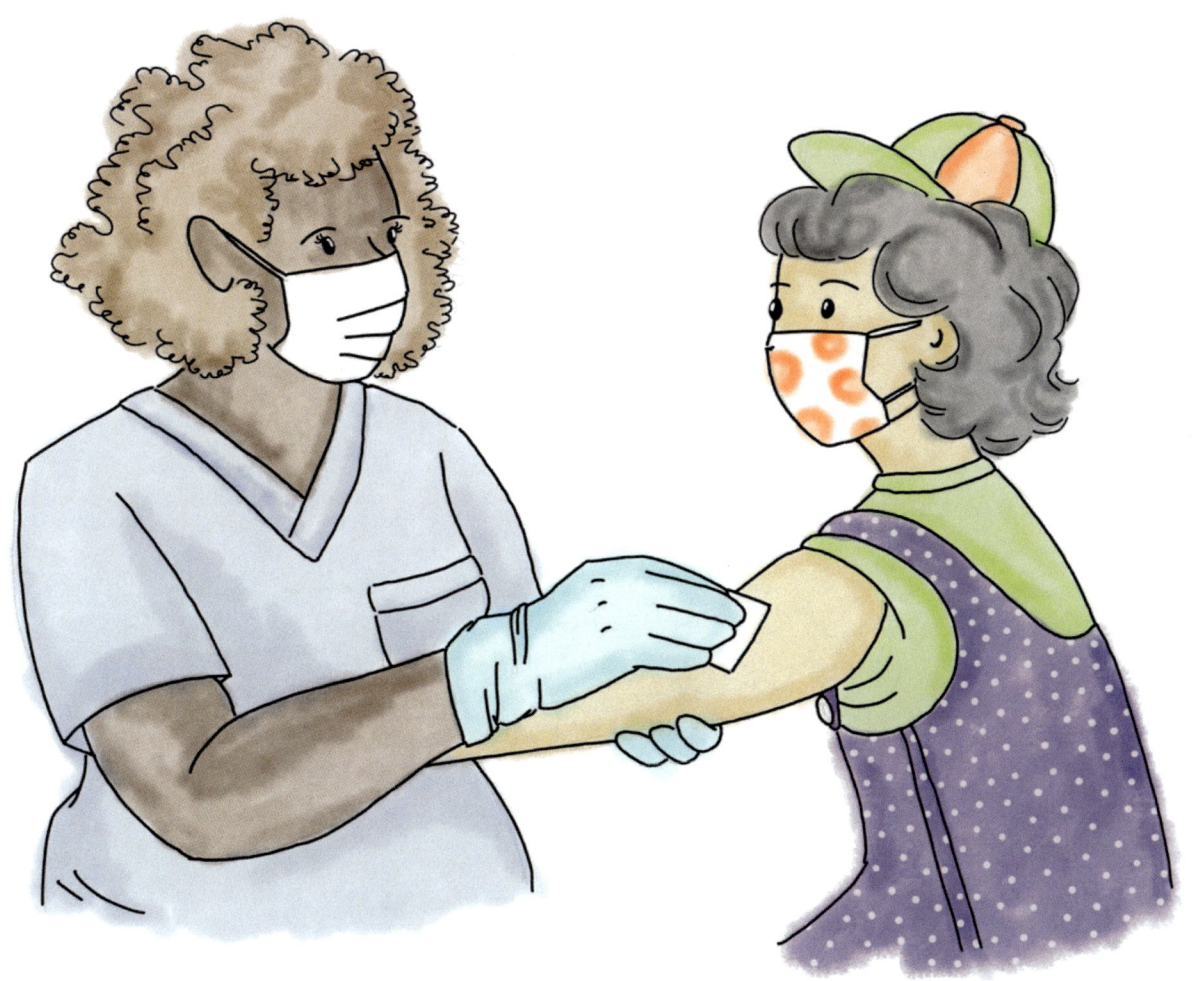

Dad says the only time I don't need to give consent is when it's touch to keep me healthy or to save me from danger.

Gold star number three:
Touch is something we can share.

I should always be able to talk about touch.
If someone wants to hide touch
I will tell them "No".

When someone has all three gold stars, that's when touch can feel like magic.

It makes me feel connected to someone else. It can help me do so many things and can make me feel full of joy.

But when someone doesn't have
the three gold stars touch can cause hurts
instead of making them better.

This hurtful touch comes in two kinds: **Snarly Touch** and **Vacuum Touch.**

Snarly like a mean old dog and Vacuum like something sucking out my joy.

Snarly Touch is when someone is angry or afraid and they lash out at someone else.

Last year Debra pushed me down in the playground and said my face looks like a pig. I scraped my elbow and my feelings were hurt.

Vacuum Touch is when someone feels sad, lonely, and empty inside and they use touch to fill the emptiness.

At our family reunion my big cousin Joe hugged me too long and too close. I felt confused and scared. He turned bright red and said we shouldn't talk about it.

 Snarly Touch and Vacuum Touch hurt other people, sometimes for a very long time.

Mom and Dad told me to talk to them about any touch that hurts my body or my feelings, or makes me feel strange or bad.

Lucky for me I have a Trust Team. I told Mom and Dad about Debra and Joe. They were proud of me that I told them and they made me feel lots better.

But it took until my birthday
to feel all the way better.

I'm glad I know about the three gold stars;

"Trust, Consent, We Can Share Touch".

They make touch full of joy and healing power.

Dancing with my friend Jeanne is so much fun! We spin in circles holding hands until we laugh and roll in the grass.

When Jeanne moved to another city
I was very sad. Cole saw how sad I was
and he ruffled my hair and gave me
a piggyback ride.

I love to snuggle with Mom when we look at the stars. When I watched a scary movie and I couldn't sleep, she curled up in bed with me.

Dad sometimes massages my shoulders and it feels so good! When he comes home from work he gives me the biggest and best hug.

I know that my Mom was giving me powerful magic when she held me after I was born. And I know that my Dad and Grandpa's touch magic was extra strong, holding hands when Grandpa was very sick.

POWERFUL MAGICAL TOUCH

It was pure love under the three gold stars.

Here's a space for your own touch drawing.

TAIMANI EMERALD REED

Taimani Emerald of Emerald Creative is the creator of whimsical illustrations that are changing the world.
As seen in major publications, including *Huffpost* & *Good Morning America*, Taimani uses her unique artistic voice to create illustrations that teach a message of kindness, anti-racism, and community empowerment to people of all ages. Her commitment to changing the world of anti-racist education spurred the activation of The World Changers Program, which donates community-sponsored art to classrooms all over The United States of America.

KIM MAGRAW

Kim Magraw has been a Licensed Massage Therapist since 2009 and is a practitioner and owner at Concordia Wellness in Portland, Oregon. Kim is inspired by issues pertaining to mental and behavioral health including as they relate to our need for caring physical contact "from our first day until our very last." He believes that nurturing emotional intelligence in children and adults is essential to developing a mature and compassionate society. It was an honor for Kim to bring this book to life in collaboration with Taimani Emerald Reed and the team at Casasola Editores.

Printed in USA for Casasola Editores
MMXXII

Made in the USA
Las Vegas, NV
12 September 2023